VOICES

TAH

50 YEARS
1924-1974

INTERNATIONAL PUBLISHERS New York

VOICES FROM WAH'KON-TAH

CONTEMPORARY POETRY of NATIVE AMERICANS

Edited by Robert K. Dodge and Joseph B. McCullough
With a foreword by Vine Deloria, Jr.

Copyright Acknowledgements

The poems in this book are copyrighted by the authors, or their publishers, or representatives who have graciously given their permission for use here. None of these poems may be reprinted without permission except by reviewers quoting passages in reviews. The biographical notes are also included in this copyright notice.

In addition, the publishers are grateful for the specific permissions granted by the following institutions and publications: *Dacotah Territory* for Marnie Walsh's "Vickie" and "Bessie Dreaming Bear"; the *Institutes of American Indian Arts*, A Bureau of Indian Affairs School, Santa Fe, N.M. for the poems of Janet Campbell, Ramona Carden, Grey Cahoe, Phil George, Bruce Ignacio, King D. Kuka, Littlebird, Charles C. Long, Alonzo Lopez, David Martinez, Calvin O'John, Agnes Pratt, Ronald Rogers, Loyal Shegonee, Liz Sohappy, Soge Track, and Donna Whitewing; *The Mustang Review* for the poems of Fred Red Cloud; the *Pembroke Magazine* for those of Ray Young Bear; the *South Dakota Review* for the poems of Paula Gunn Allen, Janet Campbell, Martha Chosa, Grey Cahoe, Patty Harjo, Bruce Ignacio, Alonzo Lopez, Duane W. McGinnis, Emerson Blackhorse Mitchell, Simon Ortiz, Norman Russell, Loyal Shegonee, Liz Sohappy, Soge Track, Winifred Fields Walters, Archie Washburn, and James Welch; *Grove Press* for Ted Berrigan's poem; and *The Prairie Schooner* for two poems by Duane W. McGinnis.

Library of Congress Cataloging In Publication Data
Dodge, Robert K   comp.
Voices from Wah'Kon-Tah.
1. American poetry—Indian authors. 2. American poetry—20th century. I. McCullough, Joseph B., joint comp. II. Title.
PS591.155D6   811'.5'408   74-1321
ISBN 0-7178-0416-X
ISBN 0-7178-0417-8 (pbk.)

Printed in the United States of America

Wah' Kon-Tah is the "Great Mystery," the sum total of all things, the conception of an impersonal, spiritual and life-giving power. The Dakotas believe that there are two kinds of songs: songs made by people, and songs that come in visions through the spirits of *Wah' Kon-Tah*. It is from the voices of *Wah' Kon-Tah* that people gain spiritual power and wisdom.

There are many other names among the various Indian peoples —Wakonda, Wakan-tanka, Nesaru, Manito—that signify the same meaning as *Wah' Kon-Tah*.

Contents

Foreword

American Indians have been denied the chance to pass through the decades of history as an experiencing community of souls capable of transforming themselves into the possibilities which confront them. The Indians of today, the intrepid spirits who captured Alcatraz and defied the greatest military power on earth at Wounded Knee, remain as ghosts with little or no immediate identity, hidden in the shadows of the past. As they gather for a final stand the clouds of warriors past, Chief Joseph, Crazy Horse, Sitting Bull, Geronimo, Dull Knife, blot them out from the hundreds of anthologies that gallop past in the noon sun of popularity.

Denied the inherent right of national existence, American Indians can only do what the forgotten peoples of the past have done and preserve in song and poetry the suffering and strife of their existence. It is thus that we have this book, this effort to grasp from the fantasy-land of the white man's mind, a sense of historical being. In the poetry of the modern Indian we find a raging sense of having been and a desperate pronouncement of future being, an effort beyond nobility that calls for recognition of the humanity and nationality of Indian existence. In poetry the broken treaties and countless betrayals are overcome and the twisting coils of the law are transcended so that if there is to be no tangible existence there will be spiritual existence.

Indian poetry, like Indian art, has struggled to emerge from the stereotypes imposed on it by non-Indians who wished to see the simple and childish recitations and drawings of a creature not yet civilized but containing that possibility. The poetry of this book is not that taught in the schools and does not follow the patterns of formal existence. It is no more and no less than what would have naturally emerged from the experience of Indian existence had there been no white man to confront. It is awareness tempered with reflection and the holiness of history as it has been experienced.

Indian poetry may not say the things that poetry says because it does not emerge from the centuries of formal western thought. It is not, one can easily discern, descriptive. It has no formula for living. It is hardly chronological and its sequences relate to the integrity of the circle, not the directional determination of the line. It encompasses, it does not point.

One faces, in fact, a desperation in presenting a foreword to any book of Indian poetry because of the experiences of the past. The white man, it seems, refuses to make that final transition from his European past and to confront the continent and its people. He rather extracts what he feels is not harmful to himself or what can be profitably used, and hurriedly passes on, unable to lay down roots, unable to reflect, and most tragically of all, unable to savor experiences.

It is with great and tragic pleasure, therefore, that I write a foreword to this book. My greatest fear is that it will be taken as books on Indians by Indians are taken—as "quaint." Within this poetry by the best of the young Indian poets is contained a fearful effort to bridge the gap between Chief Joseph and Russell Means, the leader of the Wounded Knee protest. It is a lyrical attempt to provide a transition between the glorious past with which we all agree and the desperate present which Indians know and which the white man refuses to admit. Our poets are the only ones today who can provide this bridge, this reflective statement of what it means and has meant to live in a present which is continually overwhelmed by the fantasies of others of the meaning of past events.

No essay, no slogan, no policy, no pronouncement can rescue the American Indian from his banishment to the realms of mythology by the non-Indian. Only the poet in his frightful solitude and in his ability to transcend chronological existence can build that spiritual bridge which enables individuals to travel the roads of man's experiences. Thus while we struggle with the institutions and structures of modern life and the headlines run red with anger and frustration, it is only the poets who will tell us how the battle came to its conclusion.

With the poems of this book, then, the reader is invited to savor the Indian experience. It is only in savoring that the full integrity of experience is allowed to present itself. One should not gulp one's food for it is not for energy and vitamins alone that food is eaten. It is eaten as much for future remembrances and for this reason it is savored. Once savored this poetry may brush away the years and tell you more about the Indian's travels in historical experience than all the books written and lectures given. That may be the reason that poetry seems to survive where everything else expires. That may be why these Indians still sing their songs of poetry for us.

Vine Deloria, Jr.

Acknowledgments

Any anthology such as this one could not be compiled without the assistance of a number of people who rarely receive the credit they deserve. We are especially thankful to the following: to Mrs. T. D. Allen, for permission to use much of the material and for her generous help in supplying biographical information of many of the poets; to John R. Milton, editor of *The South Dakota Review*, for his permission to use material and for supplying addresses of some of the poets; and to Vine Deloria, Jr. for writing the provocative forward to this book.

We also want to thank Susan Anderl, Special Collections Librarian at the University of Nevada, Las Vegas, for helping us in ways too numerous to mention; Pierrette Follis, for her assistance in preparing the manuscript; our wives, Leslie and Sylvia, for their inspirational and practical aid; and, of course, to all the poets whose works form the contents.

R.D., J.M.

Introduction

As much as any other racial or ethnic group, the American Indians have been the subject of stereotypes and myths that fail to perceive them in their real humanity. Deep seated prejudices and persecutions have been real dangers to their ability to survive as well as to their ability to either fully integrate into U.S. society or to preserve their own life style.

As perceived by white America the cultural image of the American Indian has been filtered through at least two important stereotypes or myths. One stereotype sees the Indian as a Noble Savage, the other as a red devil.

The stereotype of the Indian as a devil had its real beginning among the Puritans of Massachusetts, although there are foreshadowings of it in John Smith's account of Virginia, as there are also foreshadowings of the Noble Savage myth in Smith's portrayal of Pochahontas.

The Puritans saw their colonization of Massachusetts as a sacred mission. Standing in the way of that mission were dark savages who worshipped strange gods and who lived in the heart of dark forests, out of reach of the light of the sun as well as of the light of God's grace. The Puritans concluded that whatever stood in the way of their sacred mission was an obstacle set up by Satan, and that these dark men were agents of the devil. When the Puritans saw them at worship, they also decided that the Indians were worshippers of Satan.

Such an image of the Indian allowed the Puritans to look upon the Pequod war, a war in which a combined force from Plymouth and Massachusetts Bay surrounded a camp of sleeping Indians, set fire to the dwellings, killed all they could (including women and children) during the battle, killed all the captive males over the age of adolescence after the battle, and enslaved everyone else, as a mark of God's special providence. After all, this was a battle against Satan and drastic measures were called for.

The myth of the Noble Savage, on the other hand, although foreshadowed in Smith's story of Pochahontas, did not come into full flower in America until the late eighteenth and early nineteenth centuries. It was a time of slowed westward expansion, the idea of Manifest Destiny had not yet taken hold of the American imagination and there was relatively little contact between whites and reds. When such contact did take place on the frontier, it led to events similar to the Pequod war as a history of the Paxton Boys would show.

The Noble Savage myth began in Europe and spread to the cities and settled parts of America. Most of those who believed in it had seen few if any Indians. It led to the spectacle of princes, historians, writers and others travelling to the plains to ride in the buffalo hunts and to observe the pure savage. The myth, of course, grew out of the romantic tradition, and perceived the Indian as one of the few uncorrupted humans then existing.

Today, these myths still exist, and still influence the perceptions of white Americans who observe American Indians. To some extent, these myths even affect the Indians perceptions of themselves. For the readers of this book, it is important to realize that these two myths have their manifestations in white America's view of native American literature. Both myths tend to devalue the importance and the ability of native American writers.

Marlon Brando, most recently, has pointed out that we have all seen motion pictures in which the most intelligent comment made by an Indian (usually, of course, a white man pretending to be an Indian) was "Ugh!" Subtler directors or writers have more advanced Indians who are able to articulate more complex ideas such as "How?" and even "Me want firewater" and "That plenty right, Kemo sabé."

Such misconceptions of Indian speech are probably related to the myth of the Indian as a savage devil. Supposedly the Indians were "silent, sullen people incapable of articulate expression."[1]

However, according to Gerald W. Haslam, such misconceptions also result from the large differences between European and most Indian languages. Most Indian languages are agglutinative, and are pronounced relatively low and back in the mouth. The sounds,

[1] Gerald Haslam, ed. *Forgotten Pages of American Literature* (Boston, Houghton Mifflin, 1970) p. 14

according to Haslam have "a deep, throaty quality."[2]

It is easy to see, then, that to a European, a person speaking such a language would appear to be saying "Ugh," over and over, but it is important to remember that the languages of the American Indians are, in fact, capable of making the kind of distinctions that we expect of other languages.

At the other extreme, related to the myth of the Noble Savage, as well as to other misconceptions concerning Indian languages, is the belief that all American Indians are poetic. In *The Way*, Shirley Hill Witt and Stan Steiner demonstrate one of the results of this myth:

> A student at the Institute of American Indian Arts, in Santa Fe, New Mexico, was praised for his poetry. He objected: *In my tribe we have no poets. Everyone talks in poetry.* If poetry is the magical use of symbols and rhythm "to make life," as the Greeks defined it, or "to remake life," as the Cherokees say, his romanticism was realistic, at least in part. For in no segment of our society are poetry and song as religiously vital as among tribal traditionalists and modernists alike, as (the young Indian poets) attest.[3]

To be sure, in a tribal society there is a more intimate relationship between each person and the various functions of society, including the making of poetry, but to assert that everyone talks in poetry is to deny what poetry really is. It is also to deny distinctions that American Indians make between poetry and prose.

A. Grove Day attempts to distinguish between Indian poetry and Indian prose.[4] Such a distinction suggests that Indians like whites do not always speak in poetry. To believe that they do diminishes the value of the poetry that they do write or chant. The writing of poetry, as Mrs. Terry Allen long in charge of the creative writing department at the Institute of American Indian Arts seems to have successfully taught many of her students, is a difficult task that involves the measuring of rhythms, the choice of words and symbols and the shaping of it all into a unity. It is a task that many Indian poets do well.

[2] *Ibid.*, p. 15
[3] Shirley Hill Witt and Stan Steiner (eds.) *The Way* (New York, Vintage, 1972), p. 132
[4] A. Grove Day, *The Sky Clears* (Lincoln, Nebraska, University of Nebraska Press, 1970), p. 4

This is not to say that poetry does not play a large part in the everyday lives of many tribes. William Brandon points out that multivolume collections of ancient songs and chants "have been made from tiny Indian communities of only a few hundred persons."[5] Obviously, for such poems to have survived in an oral tradition within such small communities, they must have been considered important. Day points out that most of such songs and chants were religious in nature. "They attempted to get hold of the sources of supernatural power."[6] There were special songs for baking bread, for chanting over a new baby or when making its cradle, for chanting while preparing to plant seed, to indicate only a few. Thus, the integration between religion, poetry and everyday life was great, but these songs still had been already composed, committed to memory and chanted as the occasion arose. They were not made up, or talked, on demand. Thus the two predominant attitudes toward American Indians have helped to make American Indian poetry practically invisible to white America. Where such poetry has been observed, it has been largely the songs and chants of a former day that have been noticed rather than the poetry of contemporary Indians.

Two whites of some influence, however, have helped in the development of a contemporary Indian poetry and in bringing it to the attention of some white Americans. They are Terry Allen of the Institute of American Indian Arts (IAIA) and John Milton, editor of the *South Dakota Review*. Milton has devoted two issues of his review to the art and literature of the contemporary American Indian. Mrs. Allen has been in charge of the creative writing program at IAIA from its inception in 1963. Her students include about half of the poets anthologized in this book.

Looking at the IAIA poets as a group, at first glance it appears that one characteristic they have in common is a tendency toward a prosaic style, a tendency that allows such brilliant lines as Donna Whitewing's:

> "Sinister trucks prowl
>   down dim-lit alleyways."

to be followed by the vague and somewhat repetitious:

[5] William Brandon, *The Magic World* (New York, Morrow, 1971), p. xi
[6] Day, p.6

"Racing past each other,
Cars toot obscenities
Silence is crawling in open windows
Smiling and warm."

A closer look at the poems, however, together with some idea of the purposes of the IAIA will show that this group of poets is not merely prosaic, but is attempting to accomplish a serious literary purpose.

The basic idea of the IAIA is reflected in its name. It is to use traditional elements of Indian culture or art as a basis for art that will be relevant to the modern world. In literature, the traditional Indian culture is reflected in the songs and chants which have already been discussed. Many of them are repetitious and prosaic, but that is often the nature of a primitive chant.

The aim of many of the IAIA poems appears to be to transform the style of the old chants and songs into modern poetry. Some succeed more than others. Janet Campbell's "Nespelim Man," Donna Whitewing's "A Vegetable, I Will Not Be," Calvin O'John's "Dancing Teepees," Ronald Rogers' "Kindergarten," most of the poems by Emerson Blackhorse Mitchell, and many by Phil George, one of the strongest of the IAIA poets, achieve varying degrees of success in combining the ancient art form with the modern. In this way, Terry Allen's work at IAIA is rewarding. All in all, the Institute appears to be one good idea to have come out of the Bureau of Indian Affairs.

There are a number of other poets represented here besides those who come out of the IAIA, but except for Ted Berrigan they share the concern of the IAIA poets for a connection with their Indian heritage. Most of the others find it sufficient to let their subject matter show their heritage, and to draw their forms, not from the songs and chants of primitive Indians, but from the poetic forms of modern white poetry. The poems of James Welch, Marnie Walch, Simon Ortiz, Ray Youngbear, Fred Redcloud, Scott Momaday and others will seem more familiar to white readers for this reason. Yet few of these poets have achieved any notice among white editors or readers, except for John Milton and the fortunate readers of the *South Dakota Review.*

However, the content of their poems reflects their Indian heritage as effectively as the chant derived from of the IAIA poets. The forms of Welch and Ortiz, for example, are distant from one another.

Ortiz writes poems that are mainly long and somewhat loose in structure; Welch's poems are usually tightly structured; yet they are both known as poets of Indian protest, and they are both good poets.

The poems of Marnie Walch are generally narrative while those of Youngbear and Redcloud are less so. Yet all of them reflect their heritage as Indians in their poems. The themes of death, tribal ritual and the changes brought about by modern life continually reoccur. Often the poetry of some contemporary native Americans reveals the problems inherent in attempting to convey cultural awareness in a language (English) antithetical to the culture's survival. Thomas Sanders and Walter Peek remind us that "to listen for the voice out of Wah'kon-tah that drifts through the English phrasings is to hear language enriched beyond spiritual bounds."[7]

Finally, this heritage represents neither of the white stereotypes. If one wishes to continue to think of the Indian in terms of racial stereotypes, then he should not read the Indian's poetry. The Indian's poetry is one of the best ways to get to know him, and getting to know someone is one of the surest ways to beat down whatever stereotypes may have previously stood between you.

Las Vegas, Nevada   ROBERT K. DODGE
August, 1973   JOSEPH B. McCULLOUGH

---

[7] Thomas E. Sanders and Walter W. Peek (eds.) *Literature of the American Indian* (New York, Glencoe Press, 1973), p. 449

voices from WAH'KON-TAH

Paula Gunn Allen

LAMENT OF MY FATHER, LAKOTA

O many-petaled light where
stands traitorous the sign of fall,
weave basket-symbols on the autumn skull of Old Coyote.[1]
Night no longer stays the hand of cause.
What innocence could now behold our days secure,
or light could move beyond the budding tears,
(woman sign that clings to eyes
no longer comforted by grief.)

Now come to us our broken victories,
hawks mounted on the tortured wings of kill;
old age sits upon the frozen window sills
too alien for our age-dimmed sight.
And fleshless fingers touch
the careful cobwebs of our days
that hold the butterfly called morning—
turned now into the owl song of night.

I have heard it said
that such poor creatures move in every land
and cast their shadow sign on every wintered skull.
Coyote and this night

be still.
I wonder how a man can cling to life.

---

[1] Coyote, the trickster-creator, who called himself the first man, is a frequent figure in Indian mythology. According to one myth, the people discovered that the Sun must be placated by human death, or he could not move. Coyote, interpreter of signs, told the people that everyone must die. From this came the belief that death would come quickly to those who glazed on the faces of the dead.

Charles G. Ballard

NAVAJO GIRL OF MANY FARMS

Navajo girl of Many Farms
You ride on blue wings
Why do you fear?
The drop of sun
Is but my hands
Resting at your door
The desert wind
Is but my voice
Saying you are slim
Saying you are strong
The morning light
Is but my song
Singing soft to you
Ride, ride away with me
On your bright, blue wings
We will never return
Navajo girl of Many Farms

YOU NORTHERN GIRL

You northern girl, be yet
The fine sand along the River Platte
Blue flames along hickory logs
Above the ground where dancers dance

South to the yellow world
The amber world of morning lakes
Long-stemmed stillness that seldom breaks
Nor disturbs the sun's resting place

Small birds have not the wings for this
The flight across time and unlocked rhythms
Nor are they as pebbles in a stream
With colors drawn deep from wintry days

You northern girl, speak yet
Of a time of many trees, many camps of the strong
Mountain peaks that guard the fertile land
The purer light now lost to man

Though in the furnace of the Southlands
Deep in the city's web we meet
We will wing our way to the River Platte
Toward the fires of our Indian world

THE MAN OF PROPERTY

Let's let the good man sign the bill
That deprived the Indian of his will
Let's build his house upon the hill
And bring to him our misery

His children will attend the finest school
His wife will live by the golden rule
His workers for him will play the fool
And take to him our misery

His name will be on the cornerstone
He will find it proper to loan
Proper to forget the ones who groan
And take to him our misery

His fences will stretch across the land
His constituents will clap and stand
The lights will burn along the strand
Far removed from our misery

But then will come a certain day
Brothers will link arms along the way
The raging night will come to stay
And he will know our misery

During the pageant at Medicine Lodge
One bright line this—recollected but passing away,
      like a leaf that escaped the fire; it
      appears still golden, life-inhabited,
      imbued with light, with the filtered hush
      of deep forests.

During the pageant at Medicine Lodge
Later it seemed that the redman had been only a dream
      on paper, an elegant falsehood strutting
      before pioneers, a dancing image fading
      deeper into the forests, into the wild streams,
      into earth itself. They were never real!
      They sang—bird-like, bear-like, like wind,
      rustle of trees, crickets—and were no more.

During the pageant at Medicine Lodge
Conversational scraps and ideas. "A few might have
      survived," I said. I wanted to say,
      "You and I." But why stab at thin air.
      The past survives in the mind. On that
      particular day in southern Kansas *no Indians*
      were there. It was a jolly ride, it was dusty
      and hot, it was fun, but the Indians,
      whoever they were, did not arrive.

CHANGING OF THE GUARD

Why do you hold the flag so high
Old fellow of the Sac and Fox?
Those stars were never in your sky

From times past we have gone to war
Now the young are speaking new words
So be it. They have done so before

And it must come to them, the flag
If they take it from these useless hands
It must still be there, high up and strong

Grandfather, or whatever you are
You have spoken your sold-out words
To your strength I cannot reply

I know only that the time has come
When gratitude for treachery is gone
When kisses for the greedy are unclean

When I take the flag, old man
It will be but to honor the forgotten dead
Those who died for the Indian dream

Let no more be said, my son
On this matter we are of one mind
In my old time way I pass it on to you

Time was the trail went deep
From the granite ledge of the Verdigris
On west to rivers flat
And a rolling sea of grass

We followed the Arkansas to New Town
Of the Creeks and veered off
To low hills in the north
Where we camped in those final days

Having walked to never look back
Having talked to carry through
We disbanded and were no more
To choose finally is the Indian way

But time was the trail went deep
Into a green and vibrant land

NOW THE PEOPLE HAVE THE LIGHT

Now the people have the light
But time must pass, days of autumn
While the deer drink at the pool

Visions gathered by proud men
Will not affect the light, the summer rains
Must fall on a world of leaves

The swarms of small life on wings
Must find the lake, the evening birds
Bring back the songs of youth

Steaming riverbeds on the Great Plains
Must sigh for the lizard and receive
In dark sand the wayward stars

Mountain peaks high over the land
Must keep the watch through all the years
For now the people have the light

Ted Berrigan

SONNET XXIII

On the 15th day of November in the year of the motorcar
Between Oologah and Pawnee
A hand is writing these lines
In a roomful of smoky man names burnished dull black
Southwest, lost doubloons rest, no comforts drift
On dream smoke down the sooted fog ravine
In a terrible Ozark storm the Tundra vine
Blood ran like muddy inspiration: Walks he in
    around anyway
The slight film has gone to gray-green children
And seeming wide night. Now night
Is a big drink of water bugs   Then were we so fragile
Honey scorched our lips
On the 15th day of November in the year of the motorcar
Between Oologah and Pawnee

Janet Campbell

RED EAGLE[1]

Red Eagle,
Cold, dead, noble, Red Eagle.
Tomorrow they will bury you in Black Hill.
They think you have left me forever.
When I grow lonely for you
      I will walk into the night
      and listen to your brother, the wind.
He will tell me if you want me.
I will follow the path through the forest
      upon which your moccasins
      have trod so many times.
I will hear the night sounds you
      have told me about.
I will walk into the valley of Minnelosa,
      the sweet grass.
In the white moonlight I will pray.
I will pray to the spirits
      and they will speak to me
      as they have spoken to you before.
Then I will touch your tree and you
      will softly whisper to me.
From the wind, from the night, from the tree,
      from the sweet grass,
You will whisper to me,
Red Eagle, Red Eagle,
      Upon the mountain.

NESPELIM MAN²
(a song)

Ya-che-ma,³ he comes,
Ya-che-ma, he comes.
Over the mountains he comes.
Across the waters he comes.
Oh, joy, I hear him.
O, joy, I see him.

From the land of Nespelim he comes.
His mother is the sky.
His father is the earth.
He is Nespelim Man.
Oh, joy, he is Nespelim Man.
Ya-che-ma, Nespelim Man.

To Many Lakes he has come.
Let our fields be fruitful.
Let our game be plentiful.
Ya-che-ma, he goes,
Ya-che-ma, he goes.

Over the mountains he goes
Across the waters he goes.
I weep, I weep, for he is gone.
Ya-che-ma, he is gone—
     He is dead!

---

¹ Possibly a reference to William Weatherford, also known as Lamochattee or Red Eagle, a half-blood Creek Chief, born about 1870 and noted for the part he played in the Creek War of 1812-14, in which General Jackson was the leader of the American forces.
² A tribe of the Salish living on Nespelim Creek, a tributary of the Columbia.
³ Under a treaty in 1855 several tribes were incorporated under the name Yakima. The name means "The Runaway."

Ramona Carden

THE MOCCASINS OF AN OLD MAN

I hung you there, moccasins of worn buckskin.
I hung you there and there you are still.
I took you from the hot flesh of a swift buck.
I took you to my woman.

She tanned you with buck brains.
She cut and sewed and beaded.
I wore you with pride.
I wore you with leaping steps over many grounds.

Now, I sit here and my bones are stiff with many winters.
You hang there and I shall sit.
We shall watch the night approach.

TUMBLEWEED

I stood in the shelter of a great tree,
Hiding from the wind that galloped over the land.
Robbing, and wrecking, and scattering. It soared.
I was earth bound.
It tugged at the leaves,
At the grass, at things not tied.
At me.
Urging, pulling, laughing in my ear.
I listened but stood.
Flitting away, it spied a tumbleweed
and coaxed it from its roots.
The brown weed soared
and became part of the wind.
Suddenly, with a wild yearning,
I ran stumbling, with arms outstretched.
It flew on beyond me.
It stopped.
The wind flew around me,
Leaving me there.

Martha Chosa

DRUMS

Throbbing—all I can hear!
Why can't there be bells,
with floating voices
over all our dry land?
Is it going to rain?
Or is that my people
need to dance more often?
Perhaps the Sky
is watching us with anger.
Are people talking behind his back?
Suppose he's sad
of not having enough power
to drop blessing on the land,
on my people,
on my crops,
on my animals?
People! People! People!
Brothers and sisters!
Let us give pride to the Sky;
help him to send
blessing for our needs.
Leave your drums.
Let him be proud of his powers.
Great Spirit!
Now is the time to have joy.

Great Sky!
It is time to see drops
of rain and of blessing
on our dry land.

Grey Cohoe

THE FOLDING FAN

The wild beauty of an eagle, once born to virgin sky
    now held in a sacred fan.
                                Beaded feathers
stiffen the grasp, the fingers that curled
to ease the cold soul but let the agony tear,
    for the heart will weep all the same.
Never again is life made vivid
    or for who else the kind warmth?
Maybe this I know, that it is for the dying,
whose ending breaths I hear not, as the wisdom
                              will come no more,
    only to grave, olden with age.
Eternity flies now on the wings of the gone soul,
                        never to be seen.

    Listen,
a drum I hear, distance, yet;
      it's from the folding fan.
            The preying bird of death is waiting,
                calling.

Phil George

OLD MAN, THE SWEAT LODGE[1]

"This small lodge is now
The womb of our mother, Earth,
This blackness in which we sit,
The ignorance of our impure minds.
These burning stones are
The coming of new life."
I keep his words near my heart.

Confessing, I recall my evil deeds.
For each sin, I sprinkle water on fire-hot stones,
The hissed steam is sign that
The place from which Earth's seeds grow
Is still alive,
He sweats,
I sweat.

I remember, Old Man heals the sick,
Brings good fortune to one deserving.
Sacred steam rises;
I feel my pores give out their dross.
After I chant prayers to the Great Spirit,
I raise the door to the East.
Through this door dawns wisdom.

Cleansed, I dive into icy waters.
Pure, I wash away all of yesterday.
"My son, Walk in this new life.
It is given to you!
Think right, feel right,
Be happy."
I thank you, Old Man, the Sweat Lodge.

[1] The sweat lodge was almost universal for all tribes north of Mexico. It was usually a small round house made of sod, sticks or hide; an individual entered and hot rocks and water were placed inside to cause steam. After remaining for a time, he would then plunge into snow or cold water. The sweat lodge was used for religious purposes, to purify onself as well as to cure disease. Special rituals were also conducted there.

NIGHT BLESSING

Sleep plays hide-and-seek with darkness.
In reverence
All earth stands, head bowed.
Long-needled evergreens cease to
Proclaim hushed hymns of awe.
Between praise stanzas,
Night birds pause to listen,
While sending their magnetic fragrance,
The sweetness for this royalty,
Spring flowers in carpet hues
Halt their prancing dance.
Stars shoot through space
To herald Full Moon's entrance.

Within my tepee
I cannot remain on robes and blankets.
Far out into the still of night,
My heart goes forth.
I must stand in honor, respect,
One beside a tepee shadows
Gazing toward snow-capped mountains.
I turn to face the East,
Waiting to receive
Her blessing.
"Oh, Ruler of the Night,
May I so live that all I do in time
Is preparation for lasting peace."

Soon Dawn's mystic gaze
Moves toward me,
Falling upon each creature.
I raise yearning arms
And stand naked

Within Her sacred view.
Devotion surges in me
Overflows my littleness
And I must praise
In song and dance.
I am clothed in joy.
I am warmed, protected.
Content, I sleep.

ASK THE MOUNTAINS

Here I stand
For centuries watching
Moccasined trails
Wear down into
Paved highways.
Innumerable winter snows
Have robed me and
My sister—
Mother Earth.
To this moist
Green valley,
The Land of Winding Waters—
I give the beauty of
Purple peaks pointing.
From long ago
I have towered—
Unafraid.
Guarding ancient
Bits of wisdom
Learned by men and creatures.
To all inhabitants of this
New Switzerland,
The Mighty One
Smiles sunshine—
Together in happiness
We protect, provide.
In gaiety, liberty,
I saw the Nez Perce
Freely worship.
Pure as my
Glacial Waters,
Proud as the bull Elk
They lived—

Seeking to survive
Within my shadow.
I helped establish these
Intelligent, ritualistic
People—a powerful race.
I admire their
Love for life.
From tribal burial grounds,
I have seen
Peace die and
Violence invade,
I know all truth.
I am Wallowa of the
Blue Mountains.

They said, "You are no longer a lad."
    I nodded.
They said, "Enter the council lodge."
    I sat.
They said, "Our lands are at stake."
    I scowled.
They said, "We are at war."
    I hated.
They said, "Prepare red war symbols."
    I painted.
They said, "Count coups."
    I cringed.
They said, "Desperate warriors fight best."
    I charged.
They said, "Some will be wounded."
    I bled.
They said, "To die is glorious."
    They lied.

Patty Harjo

MUSINGS

Walk proud, walk straight, let your thoughts race
with the blue wind, but do not bare your soul to
your enemies.

The black mountain lion called night devours the
white rabbit of day. And the icy wind blows
over the still-warm, brown earth.

In restless dreams I called out his name,
Waking, I do not remember.

In my score of years
I have known not love
except wind, earth and darkness.

Bruce Ignacio

LOST

I know not of my forefathers
nor of their beliefs
For I was brought up in the city.
Our home seemed smothered and surrounded
as were other homes on city sites.
When the rain came
I would slush my way to school
as though the street were a wading pool.
Those streets were always crowded.
I brushed by people with every step,
Covered my nose once in a while,
Gasping against the smell of perspiration on humid days.
Lights flashed everywhere
until my head became a signal, flashing on and off.
Noise so unbearable
I wish the whole place would come to a standstill,
leaving only peace and quiet

And still, would I like this kind of life? . . .
The life of my forefathers
who wandered, not knowing where they were going,
but just moving, further and further
from where they had been,
To be in quiet,
to kind of be lost in their dreams and wishing,
as I have been to this day,
I awake.

King D. Kuka

"A TASTE OF HONEY"

True: nor love or loving is ultimate.
A doe, free in the valley,
    that but her head concealed by green,
    hoofs cleansed by artesian waters,
Is harnessed by love that shuns her.
While beauty slumbers, tonight love travels afar.

Love is nay but thatching in a storm,
    for a wind tears damp and cold,
    cruel and ruthless.
A fallen traveler like weather-beaten gaff
    shall sink, rise, sink, rise, thrice sink,
    rise ne'er from love experienced in icy depths.
The thickened lung is so with breath,
Not satisfaction of love.

Love is peace, yet it is mortal.
Plead release.
Console yourself with sorrow;
Tantalized you shall be by love.
Treasure love's memory.
Sell it to tears, regret, self-pity.
Love's outstretched arms seek to destroy you.

Love is the venom of a reptile;
A wasp, fitter to kill than keep.

Within the venom dwells death;
Without is honey.
Gamble carelessly venom's deadly game
    and you'll be dealt a losing hand.
Carefully give, and in return
Will be "a taste of honey."

Littlebird

DEATH IN THE WOODS

Corn swaying in the rhythm of the wind—
    Graceful ballerinas,
    Emerging at the edge of the forest.
All dip and dance;
    Wind tunnels through long silken hair,
    Golden teeth-seeds.
Trees chatter nervously
    Awakening sky in fright,
    Pointing at Woodman.
A mighty thud! Blow leaves deep scar;
    He strikes again . . .
Corn mourns, golden tears,
    Bows, praying for fallen brother.
Jay mocks the greedy beast
    Who has doomed majestic brother,
    His life home.
Wind tosses leaves aside as
    Woodman tramps on his way,
    Ax dripping oak's blood.
The forest, damp and silent,
    Mourning for lost Oak.
    And now remains but a
    Chirp of a lonely cricket and

Silhouette of Woodman,
Diminishing,
beyond the
saddened hill
as the far
sun sinks.

Charles C. Long

YEI-IE'S CHILD[1]

I am the child of the Yei-ie.
Turquoise for my body, silver for my soul,
I was united with beauty all around me.
As turquoise and silver, I'm the jewel
      of brother tribes and worn with pride.
The wilds of the animals are also my brothers.
The bears, the deer, and the birds are a part
      of me and I am a part of them.
As brothers, the clouds are our long, sleek hair.
The winds are our pure breath.
As brothers, the rivers are our blood.
The mountains are our own selves.
As brothers, the universe is our home and
      in it we walk
With beauty in our minds,
With beauty in our hearts, and
With beauty in our steps.
      In beauty we were born.
      In beauty we are living.
      In beauty we will die.
      In beauty we will be finished.

---

[1]Yei or Yeibichai is one of the most ancient of the Navajo gods. Like the gods of the ancient Greeks, they are conceived of as partly human.

Alonzo Lopez

DIRECTION

I was directed by my grandfather
To the East,
    so I might have the power of the bear;
To the South,
    so I might have the courage of the eagle;
To the West,
    so I might have the wisdom of the owl;
To the North,
    so I might have the craftiness of the fox;
To the Earth,
    so I might receive her fruit;
To the Sky,
    so I might lead a life of innocence.

THE LAVENDER KITTEN

Miles and miles of pasture
    rolled on before me.
Covered with grass and clover
    dyed pink, white, and blue.
At the edge of the fluctuating
    sea of watercolors
Sat a lavender kitten.
Its fur glinted from an oscillating
    ray of pink.
Quivered gently at the touch of a
    swirling blue breeze.
Its emerald eyes glittered
And gazed blindly at the lighting
    and fading sky of hazy red,
Yellow, white, and blue.
My heart knocked within my chest.
I must have the lavender kitten!
I ran across the multi-colored field,
    my arms reaching forward.
Time slowed.
I tried to run faster
    but moved twice as slowly.
The blue breeze circled and tightened
    around me,
Holding me back.
The kitten rose and stretched
    sending lavender mist
Swimming in every direction.
It turned and started away
    in huge, slow strides.

I followed and,
	by a shimmering prism lake,
I came within reach of the kitten.
I offered my hand
	and the kitten edged away,
Farther and farther.
The lake turned from crystal
	to deep purple.
I looked around.
The colors began to melt.
The red sun turned to dull gray.
The color-filled sky turned to black.
The grass and clover began
	to wither and die.
I looked down into the pool before me,
There, at the bottom of
	the orchid glass cage,
Lay the lavender kitten.

I AM CRYING FROM THIRST

I am crying from thirst.
I am singing for rain.
I am dancing for rain.
The sky begins to weep,
　　　for it sees me
　　　singing and dancing
　　　on the dry, cracked
　　　earth.

David W. Martinez

NEW WAY, OLD WAY

Beauty in the old way of life—
The dwellings they decorated so lovingly;
A drum, a clear voice singing,
And the sound of laughter.

You must want to learn from your mother,
You must listen to old men
    not quite capable of becoming white men.
The white man is not our father.
While we last, we must not die of hunger.
We were a very Indian, strong, competent people,
But the grass had almost stopped its growing,
The horses of our pride were near their end.

Indian cowboys and foremen handled Indian herds.
A cowboy's life appealed to them until economics and
    tradition clashed.
No one Indian was equipped to engineer the water's flow
    onto a man's allotment.
Another was helpless to unlock the gate.
The union between a hydro-electric plant and
Respect for the wisdom of the long-haired chiefs
Had to blend to build new enterprises
By Indian labor.

Those mighty animals graze once more
        upon the hillside.
At the Fair appear again our ancient costumes.
A full-blood broadcasts through a microphone
        planned tribal action.
Hope stirs in the tribe,
Drums beat and dancers, old and young, step forward.

We shall learn all these devices the white man has,
We shall handle his tools for ourselves.
We shall master his machinery, his inventions, his skills,
        his medicine, his planning;
But we'll retain our beauty
And still be Indians!

THIS IS TODAY

This is today,
Within walking distance of the waterhold,
Oil wells pump around the clock,
    and it is less than a day's drive
    to where factories build missiles
    and rockets and space-age hardware.
This is today
    but it has not yet come to those Navajos
    who take their domestic water
    from waterholes, and haul it
    in horse-drawn wagons
    to mud-walled hogans.
This is today.
It makes a beautiful picture
    Provided the viewer's water
    is piped into his home,
    and the vehicle that brings him
    to Navajo land
    is pulled by a three-hundred-horse-power
    engine.
This is today.
    but the Navajos are not to be pitied
They who drink the brown water
    and ride the wagons
    find beauty in this scene.
This is their wealth
This is today.

Duane W. McGinnis

INDIAN PRAYER

Memory breaks
like a stream of geese
along the edge of sunset.
The river in the clouds
heavy on the children's eyes
cools the cedar sun.

The old men balance
their thin shadows
with smoke rings
that silence the gods.

Questions for dead brothers
disappear in the river
below the centuries-old bridge
like cast-away shields.

The heavy waterbaskets
the women dip into the river
fill the evening
with lost dances
to Thunderbird.[1]

Seeing the ancestors' canoe
with ferns and Indian pipes
rooting from its past,
children call the guardian spirits
from the river forests.

Moccasins pound tribute.
The dancers cascade the vision
of their father's old defeats
by gods.

---

[1] In Indian mythology, the Thunderbird is the answer to what causes lightning and thunder. The general conception is that there is a great bird in the sky and when he flaps his wings, you will hear thunder. If you are hit by lightning and live, you are considered to have some mystical powers. The thunderstorm itself is supposed to be a contest between the Thunderbird and a giant serpent.

Animal spirits of Lapush clip past the returning train.
The child on the beach watches his father
and brothers throw fishnets on roofs to dry.
Ancient whalers, harpoons, and a black rattle
are faces that flicker in the fire.

Morning walks in rain, drifting mounds of man,
and the cry of a sea bird, garoo, garoo
diminishes the stone steps to the sea.
Only cars lurch forward on freeways like shrill tops.

Slowing down with the train, the snow in the light
rattles the linear seasons that bring the eyes
to the shaman's[1] world inside the missing flake.
The shaman throws white dust to the wind;

the rain storms for weeks in the cities.

[1] A priest or medicine man who is supposed to have special healing power and who gets his power from another world. The Shaman is the spiritual leader of a tribe.

SONG FOR YELLOW LEAF MOON

I.

Night blues as abstract as the ninth
day of yellow leaf moon—
the autumn season starts with September willows.
Life slows to a complicated new dusk—

dinner flies call the dreamer
to the door; walk up and down the screen
like planetary ghost.

On the porch, I am no longer sure
the guests sound their origins.
I offer them water, honey,
the companionship of a brief Bach cantata,
but nothing more. After dinner,
after reading a book, I realize one
void merely empties into the main current,
green and vocal and an allegory of algae.

The ocher light in the square room
suggests I put my eyes
down to rest, clear my throat quietly.

II.

The red bird in the window
screams for a long silence
as if the strangers next door
had locked their doors,
sealed off the music.
With a little effort
at crossing the room, I begin
to understand my figure in the landscape.

The wind raised the secrets
blackbirds toss like acorns.
The coughing, cloudy shadow retreats.
Learning to be buoyant, rhythmical,
humble as a reed
is what the scarecrow calls
earth's yellow meditation.

III.

Here within the circle
I watch for myths from my ancestors,
sleep before I speak
to my love of walking
on the yellow leaves,
walking the streets in zigzag
patterns before the next moon
lets me go, and opens.

Emerson Blackhorse Mitchell

MIRACLE HILL

I stand upon my miracle hill,
   Wondering of the yonder distance.
Thinking, When will I reach there?

I stand upon my miracle hill.
The wind whispers in my ear.
I hear the songs of old ones.

I stand upon my miracle hill.
   My loneliness I wrap around me.
It is my striped blanket.

I stand upon my miracle hill
   And send out touching wishes
To the world beyond hand's reach.

I stand upon my miracle hill.
   The bluebird that flies above
Leads me to my friend, the white man.

I come again to my miracle hill.
   At last, I know the all of me—
Out there, beyond, and here upon my hill.

From *Miracle Hill: The Story of a Navaho Boy,* by Emerson Blackhorse Mitchell and T.D. Allen. Copyright 1967 by the University of Oklahoma.

THE NEW DIRECTION

This vanishing old road,
> Through hail-like dust storm,
It stings and scratches,
> Stuffy, I cannot breathe.

Here once walked my ancestors,
> I was told by the old ones,
One can dig at the very spot,
> And find forgotten implements.

Wasting no time I urged on,
> Where I'd stop I knew not,
Startled I listened to the wind,
> It whistled, screamed, cried,
"You! Go back, not this path!"

Then I recalled this trail
> Swept away by the north wind,
It wasn't for me to follow,
> The trail of the Long Walk.[1]

Deciding between two cultures,
> I gave a second thought,
Reluctantly I took the new one,
> The paved rainbow highway.

I had found a new direction.

---

[1] The Long Walk refers to one of the most tragic and pathetic episodes in the history of Anglo-Indian relations. Under the direction of General James Carleton and Colonel Christopher "Kit" Carson, the Navajo Indians of New Mexico were pursued, rounded up and driven to a wretched reservation on the banks of the Rio Pecos, in east-central New Mexico—the infamous Bosque Redondo.

Within the curved edge of quarter moon
   I was told there is a road
I must travel to meet the divine one,
   On this glittering crescent.

Awed, I tremble, enfolding tobacco
   The Almighty has given us,
To put forth our faith prayers
   Rolled in the precious smoke.

I wait in patience for the light,
   Gazing at glowing galaxies
Beyond the curve of risen silver bow.
   Silent, I sit listening.

Before me I see wrinkled old man,
   Torch in his right hand for me.
I breathe in burning leaf smoke.
   I hear waterdrum and a rattle.

Fasting through the long hours,
   I stand before the universe
I hold forth my hands four times,
   I see the Mighty One!

Within the whirling mist smoke,
   The drifting scent of cedar,
The fluffy eagle feather wakes me.
I step out into blinding space.

THE FOUR DIRECTIONS

A century and eight more years,
  Since Kit Carson rode from four directions,
Deep into the heart of nomadic Navahos,
  Burning, ravishing the Land of Enchantment.

Prairie grasses are once more
  Growing as high as the horse's belly.
Cradles of wrapped babies in colors
  Of the rainbow again span the land.

I know my people will stand and rise again.
  Now it is time.
Pollen of yellow grain,
  Scatter in the four directions.

N. Scott Momaday

THE BEAR

What ruse of vision,
escarping the wall of leaves,
rending incision
into countless surfaces,

would cull and color
his somnolence, whose old age
has outworn valor,
all but the fact of courage?

Seen, he does not come,
move, but seems forever there,
dimensionless, dumb,
in the windless noon's hot glare.

More scarred than others
these years since the trap maimed him,
pain slants his withers,
drawing up the crooked limb.

Then he is gone, whole,
without urgency, from sight,
as buzzards control,
imperceptibly, their flight.

How shall we adorn
Recognition with our speech?—
Now the dead firstborn
Will lag in the wake of words.

Custom intervenes;
More than language means,
We are civil, something more:
The mute presence mulls and marks.

Almost of a mind,
We take measure of the loss;
I am slow to find
The mere margin of repose.

And one November
It was no longer in the watch,
As if forever,
Of the huge ancestral goose.

So much symmetry!
Like the pale angle of time
And eternity.
The great shape labored and fell.

Quit of hope and hurt,
It held a motionless gaze,
Wide of time, alert,
On the dark distant flurry.

EARTH AND I GAVE YOU TURQUOISE[1]

Earth and I gave you turquoise
      when you walked singing
We lived laughing in my house
      and told old stories
You grew ill when the owl cried
We will meet on Black Mountain

I will bring corn for planting
      and we will make fire
Children will come to your breast
      You will heal my heart
I speak your name many times
The wild cane remembers you

My young brother's house is filled
      I go there to sing
We have not spoken of you
      But our songs are sad
When Moon Woman goes to you
I will follow her white way

Tonight they dance near Chinle
      by the seven elms
There your loom whispered beauty
      They will eat mutton
and drink coffee till morning
You and I will not be there

I saw a crow by Red Rock
      standing on one leg
It was the black of your hair
      The years are heavy
I will ride the swiftest horse
You will hear the drumming hooves

[1] Turquoise has long occupied a prominent place in the mythology and folklore of the Indians of the Southwest. Indian tradition attributes many virtues to it, such as possessing the mystic power to help, protect and bring good fortune to the wearer.

PIT VIPER

The cordate head[1] meanders through himself:
Metamorphosis. Slowly the new thing,
Kindled to flares along his length, curves out.
From the evergreen shade where he has lain,
Through inland seas and catacombs he moves.
Blurred eyes that ever see have seen him waste,
Acquire, and undiminished: have seen death—
Or simile—come nigh and overcome.
Alone among his kind, old, almost wise,
Mere hunger cannot urge him from this drowse.

[1] Heart shaped

BUTEO REGALIS[1]

His frailty discrete, the rodent turns, looks.
What sense first warns? The winging is unheard,
Unseen but as distant motion made whole,
Singular, slow, unbroken in its glide.
It veers, and veering, tilts broad-surfaced wings.
Aligned, the span bends to begin the dive
And falls, alternately white and russet,
Angle and curve, gathering momentum.

[1] Buteo refers to any of a genus of large, broad-winged, soaring hawks that prey on rodents. The Buteo Regalis is one of two species of the rough-legged hawk.

Calvin O'John

DANCING TEEPEES

Dancing teepes
High up in the Rocky Mountains,
Dancing teepees
Dance on the grassy banks of Cripple Creek
With laughing fringes in the autumn sun.
Indian children
Play with bows and arrows
On the grassy banks of Cripple Creek.
Indian women
Gather kindling
To start an evening fire,
Dancing teepees
Dance against fire-lighted autumn trees.
Braves returning
Home from raiding,
Gallantly ride into camp
With horses, scalps, and ornaments.
Dancing teepees,
Sleep now on the grassy banks of Cripple Creek
High up in the Rocky Mountains.

Simon Ortiz

TEN O'CLOCK NEWS

berstein disc jockey
telling about indians
on ten o'clock news
o they have been screwed
i know everybody's talking
about indians yesterday
murdering conquest the buffalo
in those hills in kansas
railroad hustling progress
today maybe tomorrow in
ghost dance dreams we'll
find out berstein doesn't know
what indians say these days
in wino translations
he doesn't know that and even
indians sometimes don't know
because they believe in trains
and what berstein tells them
on ten o'clock news

THIS PREPARATION

these sticks i am holding
i cut down at the creek.
i have just come from there.
i listened to the creek
speaking to the world,
i did my praying,
and then i took my knife
and cut the sticks.
there is some sorrow in leaving
fresh wounds in growing things,
but my praying has relieved
some of my sorrow. prayers
make things possible, my uncle said.
before i left i listened again
for words the creek was telling,
and i smelled its smell which
are words also. and then
i tied my sticks into a bundle
and came home, each step a prayer
for this morning and a safe return.
my son is sleeping still
in this quietness, my wife
is stirring at her cooking,
and i am making this preparation.
i wish to make my praying
into these sticks like gods have taught.

now that i have lighted my smoke
i am motioning to the east
i am walking in thought that direction
i am listening for your voices
i am occurring in my mind
          this instance that i am here
now that i have breathed inwards
i am seeing the mountains east
i am travelling to that place of birth
i am aware of your voices
i am thinking of your relationship with me
          this time in the morning that we are together
now that i have breathed outwards
i am letting you take my breath
i am moving for your sake
i am hearing the voices of your children
i am not myself but yourself now
          at this time your spirit has captured mine
now that i am taking breath in again
i have arrived back from that place of birth
i have travelled fast and surely
i have heard what you wanted me to hear
i have become whole and strong with yourself

          this morning i am living with your breath.

RELOCATION

don't talk to me no words
don't frighten me
for i am in the blinding city
the lights
the cars
the deadened glares
     tear my heart
     and close my mind
who questions my pain
the tight knot of anger
in my breast
i swallow hard and often
and taste my spit
and it does not taste good
who questions my mind

i came here because i was tired
the BIA taught me to cleanse myself
daily to keep a careful account of my time
efficiency was learned in catechism
the sisters spelled me good in white
and i came here to feed myself
corn and potatoes and chili and mutton
did not nourish me it was said
so i agreed to move
i seem walking in sleep
down streets down streets grey with cement
and glaring glass and oily wind
armed with a pint of wine

i cheated the children to buy
i am ashamed
i am tired
i am hungry
i speak words
i am lonely for hills
i am lonely for myself

Agnes Pratt

DEATH TAKES ONLY A MINUTE

Agonies of change
can be heard
in the lonely silence
of a single raindrop
bending a leaf downward.

All this is distant
and will fade further back
when my relatives assemble to haggle
over the price of dying.

EMPATHY

Our glances spin silver threads,
Weaving a web of closeness;
Catching, holding
A love too tenuous for words.
Woven and remembered
In silence, those hours
When time had something
To do with the moon.

Stay, or flee
As you must—
Uncountable the ways
We seek ourselves
I will keep
The interwoven strands of you
As I keep the enduring moon
And its web of shadow.

Fred Red Cloud

A TALE OF LAST STANDS

His hair was yellow and long
    and shone like singing hills
    There were times when he
    spoke as our friend
    and waved the branch of peace.

But the night in the Metropolitan Hotel
    when he wrote the unremembered
    truth that his ambition
    trampled old words into dust,
    the night he threw splinters
    of justice onto the floor and
    promised death to Sitting Bull,

That night he lost his name
    of honor with my people.
    What was to be his ambush
    of us, turned out to be
    our ambush of him.

Now the tumbleweeds blow down
    cemetery rows of Indian
    and trooper. Little streams
    wander restlessly in the
    low hills and yesterdays
    blur into sluggish tomorrows.

Rain and wind and sun
  float leisurely over the
  land of the Little Big Horn
  and the wild duck's cry
  drifts down from eternal heghts.

My people felt the shock of
  national defeat in battles
  that followed. Our war shirts
  were hung on prison walls,
  and reservations fused us into
  a sleep-muddied people.

The heel of time walked on
  and now the white man
  watches the mountain waters
  crash against his empire.

I sit with eyes like brown wounds
  and remember a yellow-haired laugh
  in a place where
  tumbleweeds blow
  and I think of Dien Bien Phu,
  and Belgian Congo, other Aryan
  last stands, sacrificial totem games,
  and a bitter laugh
  sprawls across my memory-wrinkled face.

Now . . . others ride the black-bones
  horse of sorrow
  as I watch from the shadows of time.

MACHU PICCHU, PERU[1]

A railroad suddenly hops out of the
        quartz mountain. Edges of time
        explode at the eyes, painful as
        a child's nightmare. Double-jointed
        rivers stretch toward purple,
        cantilevered mountains honed
        by the leather sky as the steam
        engine coughs like a widow in
        church. 12,000 feet. Cuzqueno
        Indian babies sit straight as
        daisies. An airplane stutters
        overhead. A net of sky falls
        on the hardness of speed here,
        near the fabled Bridge of
        San Luis Rey.

Below . . . a stone shelf holding an
        offering, a small inn, fragile as
        first frost. The sky becomes a
        beggar, leans forward and holds out
        an alms bowl. My ears crack with
        the sharpness of a spine of clay
        in a Lima potter's hand. Height
        soaks away. We are where lizards
        play in the ruined stone of
        Machu Picchu. Smells of history.
        are copper at the nose, here,
        where Angels fall. My feet touch
        the 3000-stone path of Inca princes
        and fairy tales dribble from the
        mouths of the betel-stained guides.

[1] An ancient fortress city in the Peruvian Andes, about 50 miles northeast of Cuzco.

Ronald Rogers

TAKING OFF

1
Barely did the dust settle
huddle down
than the wind blew
kicked it up
slapped me right in the eyes.

"Oh, Hell," I said.

2
The dust sits on everything
everyone
on the streets
on everyone
I blow (whew)
to clean them off.

They cloud up.

3
I stuff my bag
full of clothes
the road is dusty
the road sign is dusty
my thumb is dusty
I blink.

Somebody gives me a ride.

4

The car starts up
we're off
the road is smooth
zump zump zump
go the white paint lines
beneath us.

I feel superior.

5

The driver asks me
"Where are you going?"
"Beg pardon?" I say
The driver laughs
slaps my back
the dust blooms up
I cough.

I tell him to stop the car.

6

I am sitting on my bag
I sigh
I put out my thumb
zzem
goes a car.
The dust swirls up.

KINDERGARTEN

In my kindergarten class
there were windows around the room
and in the morning we all took naps.
We brought our own rugs and crayons
because that was responsibility
and we learned to tell the colors apart.

Sometimes we read stories
about wrinkled old pirates with parrots
who talked about cities of gold.
And then we'd talk about cities of gold
with streets of silver
and we'd laugh and laugh and laugh.

The floors were all made of wood
in long, long strips—
brown wood with un-peely wax.
One day the toughest kid in school
got mad and yelled at the teacher
and we smiled when he went to the principal.

The principal had a long black whip
studded through with razor blades
and nine lashes on it.
The principal wore a black suit
and smoked Pall Malls
and wrote bad notes to your father.

In my kindergarten class
there were windows around the room
and in the morning we all took naps.
We brought our own rugs and crayons
because that was responsibility
and we learned to tell the colors apart.

Norman H. Russell

THE EYES OF THE CHILD DO NOT SEE ME

i look into the eyes of the child
the eyes of the child do not see me
the eyes of the child look somewhere else

i look down at the sand
the child has a stick in his hand
the child makes pictures in the sand

what do the pictures mean?
what do the eyes of the child see?

i speak to the child
i ask him what he draws in the sand
the child looks at me and says nothing

the child arises and runs into the forest
i sit still looking a long time at his pictures
something in the sand is speaking to me.

THE WORLD HAS MANY PLACES
MANY WAYS

in the forest hearing
the anger of the black and yellow
wasp in the old tree going
down the sky to the eating
mouth of the earth i walk
a new path around i cannot
speak friend words to
this creature who
only speaks war

in the black night coming
out of the black lake water
mists of mosquitoes seeking
blood of my body i cover
myself with the blanket waiting
the sun of the morning which sends
the night creatures flying
into the trees and the waters
their secret homes to hide

one goes his way with wise feet
one walks with open eyes
one sleeps in his own places
the man has his place in the world
the world has many places many ways
only the creature who leaves his own place
only the creature who walks another's way
will be killed will be eaten.

THE GREAT WAY OF THE MAN

the eagle's eye is the strongest eye
the arm of the bear is the strongest arm
nothing flies so well as the swallow
nothing swims so fast as the fish
nothing runs so quick as the deer
nor leaps so far as the panther
the wolverine's teeth are the strongest teeth
the yellow wasp has the greatest poison
every animal has its one thing
every animal has its one great way

which is the great way of the man?
what is the thing that he does?

the man goes everywhere and does everything
the man sees almost as well as the eagle
the man runs almost as fast as the deer
the man swims almost as fast as the fish

the man is more cunning than the fox
the man is more cunning than all the animals
the gods of the man are more powerful
than the gods of the animals.

what does the forest do monday through friday?
i was a boy; i knew; now i have forgotten
all my dreams are dying
all my dreams are dead

i leave at night i return at night
what does the world do during the day
the world works the world works
all my dreams are dying

young girls lie on beaches young boys play
this is what the world does during the day
i read my newspaper
all my dreams are dying

i am going to a white hell there will be
typewriters typing file cases standing
secretaries with spread legs
all my dreams are dying

when i turn the television off silence comes
like a black cloak and holds me
trembling trembling
all my dreams are dead.

Bruce Severy

POEMS

my poems
are the sounds
of pigeons
feathering the moonlight.

feathering the twitch
in the eye
of a hawk
heavy with hoot sleep.

OPENING DAY

I hear ghosts of grouse
in wheat stubble
or late barley.

grouse ghosts
eat buffalo berries
and cluck.

but they never fly out.

I walk all day.

I hunt.

I hear shots banging out of empty guns.

until the sun
goes back to the lake.

I have many birds
inside me
            already.

DESERTED FARMS POEM

alone hunting.
on the hill behind
a deserted farm gone awry.
junk strewn about.
wrecked by vandals.
by Tyrkir, a mercenary, a German.
by Thorhall, later lost.
by Eirik the Red.
found Vinland: old way of saying.
astragalus.
oxytropis, maydelliana.
vetch.
locoweed.
a cow's jaw on the prairie.
teeth of the old ships
scattered around.

STRUGGLE FOR THE ROADS

prairie grass:

new sprouts
in the tire ruts
of the dirt roads.

trucks and buses
roll out the roads
like dough:

trucks and buses
and the seasons
of new dust.

but night creatures
keep reseeding
from invisible bags of seeds.

and sky gods water
from secret ponds
hidden in the stars
of the upper limbs
of the cottonwoods.

FIRST AND LAST

as the first congress
was called:
assembly of elders,
assembly of soldiers:

as the first issue of debate
was debated
against Kish, first given
after the flood:

as the first vote
was taken:
Gilgamesh voted there:

as the first sanction of war
was passed down:
and: as the war
was lost:
as all wars have been lost:

as I, chronicler,
inscribe this
in the lasting clay
of the banked Tigris:

the river that flows
first and last:
through the uneven land
of our memory.

Loyal Shegonee

LONELINESS

The deafening tic-tic-tic of the clock,
The thunder of my own thoughts rumble 'round
The dark room crowding its silence in upon me.
Where are my friends? What is there to do?
The slow steady pounding of my lonesome heart,
The never-ending thump-thump-thump of my pulse
Against a wet pillow, the only living sounds to listen to!
Visions drift slowly past my eyes . . .
Visions of scarred, contorted trees standing in barren,
                                        desolate fields . . .
Visions of solitary children standing in deserted alleys
With tears washing clean rivulets down their dirty faces . . .
Visions of old men, old women, dying with hopelessness
And agony twisted into their aged masks of death . . .
Visions of neglected tombstones crumbling by
Abandoned churches . . . Oh God!
Where are my friends?
Someone, please come and talk to me!

Liz Sohappy

ONCE AGAIN

Let go of the present and death.
Go to the place nearest the stars,
gather twigs, logs;
build a small fire,
a huge angry fire.

Gather nature's skin,
wet it, stretch it,
make a hard drum,
fill it with water
to muffle the sound.

THE PARADE

The light glows bright
as the parade begins.
Not everyone has come,
only the old ones.
The Eastern tribes came far,
dressed in cloth, wearing silver.
From the southeast trailed teared travelers
of the Five Civilized Tribes.
From the plains came buffalo hunters
dressed in beaded, fringed buckskin.
The light glows brighter
as each tribe passes.

It was such a long time ago
when he was first sighted,
running through the forest
like a frightened, swift lean deer.
When he danced in bird feathers,
dancing frenzied around blue ashes.
In the twilight of dawn, again he dances.
Drums thunder over creeks
to the swishing grasses on the plains.
Chants echo across the land of yellow maize,
along the paths of the sacred buffalo.

The years flow like running water.
Grasses grow yellow, rocks crumble to crust
as old ones come, they pass.

Soge Track

INDIAN LOVE LETTER

Lady of the crescent moon
tonight I look at the sky
You are not there
You are not mad at me, are you?
"You are angry at the people,
Yes, I know."
          they are changing
          be not too hard
If you were taken to
the mission school,
not because you wanted,
but someone thought it best for you
you too would change.

They came out of nowhere
telling us how to eat our food
how to build our homes
how to plant our crops.
Need I say more of what they did?
All is new—the old ways are nothing.
          they are changing
          be not too hard
I talk to them
they turn their heads.
Do not be hurt—you have me
I live by the old ways
I will not change.

Tonight—my prayer plumes in hand
with the white shell things—
to the silent place I will go
(It is for you I go, please be there.)
Oh! Lady of the crescent moon
with the corn-silk hair —I love you[1]
        they are changing
        be not too hard

[1] According to Navajo mythology, Hasjelti and Hostjoghon were the children of Ahsonnutli, the turquoise, and Yolaikaiason (white-shell woman, wife of the Sun). Ahsonnutli placed an ear of white corn and Yolaikaiason an ear of yellow corn on the mountain where the fogs meet. The corn conceived, the white corn giving birth to Hasjelti and the yellow corn to Hostjoghon. These two became the great song-makers of the world. They gave to the mountain of their nativity (Henry Mountain in Utah) two songs and two prayers; they then went to Sierra Blanca (Colorado) and made two songs and prayers and dressed the mountain in clothing of white shell with two eagle plumes placed upright upon the head.

Also, according to myth, when the Indians see the silk on the cornstalk they are reminded oe the beautiful woman with long light hair who has not forgotten them.

Marnie Walsh

EMMET KILLS-WARRIOR
TURTLE MOUNTAIN RESERVATION

1.
nobody know what i got inside
but i think to tell it all
how it is to be indian
on the reservation
where i was born
where i grow up
where i die

2.
i live in a government house
eat government food
go to their school
where i read about black people
live in a crowd in a city
see pictures where they all mad
at rats in their houses

3.
i would like to live in a city
i would like to get mad
at a thing like rats

4.

they told me
we take care of your mama
in government hospital
she get their funeral too
my brother at their war
my sister in their jail
i come out to the prairie
sit on old rock
i think about old days
when the indian didnt have
no government
to be born or die

5.

well that what i got inside
that my story
the government can go shit

THOMAS IRON-EYES
BORN CIRCA 1840, DIED 1919
ROSEBUD AGENCY
SO. DAK.

1.

I woke before the day, when the night bird
Knocked three times upon my door
To warn the Other Sleep was coming.
By candlelight I painted the two broad stripes
Of white across my forehead, the three scarlet spots
Upon my cheek. I greased well my braids
With sour fat from the cooking pan, then tied them
With a bit of bright string
Saved for this occasion.
From the trunk I took the dress of ceremony:
The breechclout and the elkskin shirt,
The smoke of their breath strong in my nose;
The smoke not of this time, this life or place
But of my youth, of many lodges I dwelt within,
The pony raids, the counting coup,
The chase and kill of buffalo;
The smell of grass when it was green,
The smell of coming snows
When food was plentiful within the camp
And ice crept over the rivers.
I put on the dress; then the leggings with scalps,
Now thin and colorless as the hair
Of sickly animals, sinew tied along the seams;
And on my feet the red-beaded moccasins
Worn by none but the bravest of warriors.
I lie here, my dry bones and ancient skin
Holding my old heart.
The daystar finds me ready for the journey.

2.

Another time, another life, another place,
My people would have wrapped me
In deerskin, sewed me in the finest hides;
Borne me in honor to the cottonwood bier,
Laying at my right hand the sacred pipe
And at my left the arrows and bow, the lance
I bound with thongs and hung
With the feathers from the eagle's breast.
Below the scaffold of the dead
My pony of the speckled skin and fierce heart
Would be led, and with a blow of the stone axe
Lie down to wait my needs.
Far above in the sacred hoop of the sky
Long-sighted hawks hanging on silent wings
Would mark my passing.

3.

When the Life-Giver hid from the night
The dark wind would speak to my spirit
And I would arise, taking up my weapons.
Mounting my horse I would follow
The great path over the earth, beyond the stars.
I would see the glow of cooking fires
As bright as arrow tips across the northern sky;
Waiting for me, old friends would dance and feast
And play the games of gambling.
Behind me drums would beat and willow whistles cry
Like the doves of spring who nested
In the berry bushes near the river of my village.
I would pause to hear my sons in council,
Speaking of my deeds in war, my strength and wisdom.
My woman in her sorrow would tear her clothing,
Bloody her face marked with ashes,
And with a knife cut off her plaited hair.

4.

But I am Thomas, here, where no grass grows,
Where no clear rivers run;
Where dirt and despair abound,
Where heat and rain alike rust out
The souls of my people, the roofs of tin;
Where disease like a serpent slips from house to house
And hunger sits in the dooryard.
I am Thomas. I wait for the wagon
To bring the government box of pine;
I wait for the journey to the burying ground
Below the sandy butte where rattlesnakes
Stink in burrows, and the white man's wooden trinities
Stand in crooked rows.
There I will be put beneath the earth.
They will seal in my spirit.
I will not hear the dark wind's cry
To come and take the starry road
Across the circle of the sky.

VICKIE
FORT YATES, NO. DAK.
1970

1.
i went to the dance
tommy little dog
ask me
i wait by the road
seen the red go
in the water   in the lake
then yellow spiderwebs
climb up the sky
one star watching
it get dark
tommys pickup come down the hill
i get in
saturday night is whisky night
we drink   i forget
the red sun in the water

2.
i hear
the agency hall
banging   shouting   stomping
i ready to dance
old bull-toes
put his mark
on our hands at the door
white mens music
upon the stage
christmas lights all around
one time i was the angel
up there
mama made me pretty wings

tommy was a shepherd
charlie two-head
baby jesus
he died after
i forget why

3.
well
them white mens music
just what we like
for dancing
the floor go rockarock
i got on my red dress
my beads
tommy wear his sateen shirt
purple pink
we go round and round
push push
saturday night   whisky night

4.
some old squaws
on benches next the wall
watch us
outside the old men
mostly drunk
spit on ground
drink   tell jokes
aunt nettie drunk
in her plymouth
on back seat
aunt nettie come back
to reservation
been to college
right away cecil dog-heart

give her baby
when she drunk
saturday nights
all the men get on her

5.

we all drink vodka
at my cousins truck
everybody happy
everybody feeling good
lights all dusty
i got dusty eyes
so i not see right
joshua get mad
nobody care but tommy
they fight   fall down
joshua get a thing
out of truck
hit tommy on head
too much
it get all quiet
we go away

6.

next day aunt nettie
say he dead
we dig potatoes a little
mama ask me
how i come home
if tommy dead
i say i forget
but i dont forget
when i seen the sun
all red
go in the water

SETH DISMOUNTS THRICE
RAPID CITY, SO. DAK. 1967

1.
seth dismounts thrice
caught josephine
his new wife
in somebodys bed
took his thirty-thirty carbine
got in korea
shot them dead

2.
seth had the idea
to go tell the police
but instead
went to the star-
light found denise
eagle-ear at the bar
and then she said
did he want a piece
drunk he did it drunk
in halley park
but her head broke
it went thunk
on a rock in the dark

3.
seth thinks it good joke
for some fat white
lady tourist to find
in daylight
but three times bad sign
for dumb indian buck
next day police find him
seth say it just his luck

4.

i say it sure been
one fucked up
high price night
for seth dismounts thrice

CHARLIE TWO-HEAD
WHITE SHIELD, NO. DAK.
1968

1.

my sister betty
got charlie last winter
we all like him
when he new
one day we go to town
charlie stayed to home
we all come back
betty look at him then
he got blood
coming out the nose
out the eyes
lots of flies
all around
we wash him up
he dont move any
betty dont want police
to ask questions
at night she put him
in lake

2.

it get summer again
the ice go away
people with big boats
come fishing
a white man catch charlie
thought he got big catfish
haul him in
has heart attack
i hear about it

3.

and i think
charlie full of surprise
like when betty get him
and when we find him dead
and when he got fished out
from the lake

BESSIE DREAMING BEAR
ROSEBUD, SO. DAK. 1960

we all went to town one day
went to a store
bought you new shoes
red high heels

aint seen you since

Winifred Fields Walters

NAVAJO SIGNS

How can you know, or understand, our loss
The rough-edged feel of poverty that came
to us in broken treaties' scourging hour?
Your skin is much too pale, or else too black
(Though white or colored skin is not the point).
You never lived with legend, ancient tales,
Told many times around a hogan fire
While bitter winter sapped the very flames.
You never slept an infant's passive sleep
Bound in a cradleboard, handcarved and laced
The way the Holy Ones taught us in days
Long past, beyond our farthest memory.
You never tended sheep in lambing time
Nor watched lambs frolic, stiff-kneed, in the rain.
You never knew serenity of life
In tune with nature's balanced give and take,
That total, grateful sense of solitude,
That prayer of thanks breathed out for hunter's skill,
A prayer which reaches silently to the
Great Source, as close in red rock canyons as
In rich and hallowed chapels made by men.
To you, tradition seems a binding thing,
But there are those of us who turn ourselves,
At least within our hearts, to that which was,
And was so handsomely; reluctant still

To lay away such beauty and such peace,
As brotherhood beyond the clan or tribe,
That precious dignity in which a people walked
The pollen path: that timeless way,
So simple, so complex, so nearly gone.

Archie Washburn

HOGAN

Hogan
Sitting against
The flying dust of wind.
Here and there flows the old raggy
Long johns.

UNKNOWN SMOKE

Out in the far distance away
I saw a cloud of smoke
Flowing into the gentle air,
Wondering what it was from here
Where I was standing all puzzled up,
With a sway of clean fresh air
Blowing through my black crisp hair.

Not knowing what it really was I stood
With strong sorrow break-down,
With many known and unknown voices
In the background of my image.
Looking around with astonishment it looked on my
Face among the crowds with many unknown
And known faces of the crowd.

Wishing what was happpening
In the far distance in the west,
Everything turned out clear with a siren
Sounding through the town going towards west.
The siren sounded loud and turned out with faded sound
In the distant far away.
Still the smoke floated around in the clear day.
Wondering what was happening in the distance,
I only know that it's an unknown smoke in
The far distance in the west.

James Welch

THE MAN FROM WASHINGTON

The end came easy for most of us.
Packed away in our crude beginnings
in some far corner of a flat world,
we didn't expect much more
than firewood and buffalo robes
to keep us warm. The man came down,
a slouching dwarf with rainwater eyes,
and spoke to us. He promised
that life would go on as usual,
that treaties would be signed, and everyone—
man, woman and child—would be innoculated
against a world in which we had no part,
a world of wealth, promise and fabulous disease.

ONE MORE TIME

1.

Where he really hung, there
on the tree, a promising star
and great child of wonder,
I sit in memory of yellow lights,
the fantasies of lovely aunts
at Christmas time. The Eve
astounds itself with a pale snow.

Children in their socks rush by me,
bent on odd deliveries—the promise
a child made them years ago
before we felt the twinge
of common guilt. How far
we have come, how sacred is the snow
that eats like cancer at our bones.

2.

How many women say, Child, wrap me
in your camel robe, lay me down,
spread in the straw and chaff
of all my poor loves' salvation.
Tender me, Child, one quick kiss
before your terrible road strikes off
the broad fantasies of your mother's way.

3.

I am basking in the white rain
of my father's seed. I do not wish
to come, to coat the limbs of my
father's tree a second time.
The salvation's in my bones like cancer
and I wish to die like men.

DREAMING WINTER

Don't ask me if these knives are real.
I could paint a king or show a map
the way home—to go like this:
wobble me back to a tiger's dream,
a dream of knives and bones too common
to be exposed. My secrets are ignored.

Here comes the man I love. His coat is wet
and his face is falling like the leaves,
tobacco stains on his Polish teeth.
I could tell jokes about him—one up
for the man who brags a lot, laughs
a little and hangs his name on the nearest knob.
Don't ask me. I know it's only hunger.

I saw that king—the one my sister knew
but was allergic to. Her face ran until
his eyes became the white of several winters.
Snow on his bed told him that the silky tears
were uniformly mad and all the money in the world
couldn't bring him to a tragic end. Shame
or fortune tricked me to his table, shattered
my one standing lie with new kinds of fame.

Have mercy on me. Lord, really. If I should die
before I wake, take me to that place I just heard
banging in my ears. Don't ask me. Let me join
the other kings, the ones who trade their knives
for a sack of keys. Let me open any door,
stand winter still and drown in a common dream.

HARLEM, MONTANA: JUST OFF THE RESERVATION

We need no runners here. Booze is law
and all the Indians drink in the best tavern.
Money is free if you're poor enough.
Disgusted, busted whites are running
for office in this town wise enough
to qualify for laughter. The constable,
a local farmer, plants and the jail with wild
raven-haired stiffs who beg just one more drink.
One drunk, a former Methodist, becomes a saint
in the Indian church, bugs the plaster man
on the cross with snakes. If his knuckles broke,
he'd see those women wail the graves goodbye.

Goodbye, goodbye, Harlem on the rocks,
so bigoted, you forget the latest joke,
so lonely, you'd welcome a battalion of Turks
to rule your women. What you don't know,
what you will never know or want to learn—
Turks aren't white. Turks are olive, unwelcome,
alive in any town. Turks would use
your one dingy park to declare a need for loot.
Turks say bring it, step quickly, lay down and dead.

Here we are when men were nice. This photo, hung
in the New England Hotel lobby, show them nicer
than pie, agreeable to the warring bands of redskins
who demanded protection money for the price of food.
Now, only Hutterites out north are nice. We hate
them. They are tough and their crops are always good.
We accuse them of idiocy and believe their belief all wrong.

Harlem, your hotel is overnamed, your children
are raggedy-assed but you go on, survive
the bad food from the two cafes that peddle
your hate for the wild who bring you money.
When you die, if you die, will you remember
The three young bucks who shot the grocery up,
locked themselves in and cried for days, we're rich,
help us, oh God, we're rich.

Donna Whitewing

AUGUST 24, 1963—1:00 A.M.—OMAHA

Heavy breathing fills all my chamber
Sinister trucks prowl
   down dim-lit alleyways.
Racing past each other,
   cars toot obscenities.
Silence is crawling in open windows
   smiling and warm.
Suddenly,
   crickets and cockroaches
   join in the madness:
   cricking and crawling
Here I am!
A portion of some murky design.
Writing,
   because I cannot sleep,
   because I could die here.

A VEGETABLE, I WILL NOT BE

Who would suspect, or even know
    the ivory-white innocence
    of steaming hot cake:

Not you?
Let me tell you something.
Wheat grows a pure gold coat.
Grazing is plush green plunder.
Well,
    it ought to be splendid!
Wheat, fed on bones
    for its white flesh,
    ate gold teeth from skulls
    scattered through the yard,
        for a coat.
Green grasses:
    from green flesh at full moon.
Harvesting wheat,
    a man fell dead from heart attacks.
To the Sod!
This hot cake is moist
    and steams of three tablespoons milk—
    from a dying cow.
When time stretches me to nothing,
    read instructions of my burial carefully.
It's all taped to the bottom
    of an oatmeal box—
    third cupboard to the left as you enter the kitchen,
    bottom shelf.
It reads:

"Lay me low in the wheat yards.
Fill my head with gold teeth.
I could not risk grassing to cows for milk;
Cows dry up sometimes.
I'd rather be a hot cake.
I will not be a bowl.
           of peas!"

Ray Young Bear

WRONG KIND OF LOVE

he placed the medicine
over the skillet
which held glowing ashes.
then with a blanket
he formed himself
into a small hill.
it grew each time
he inhaled. a song
followed making everything
complete: the girl who
possessed him would soon
realize the powers of
the northern medicine men.

he said, i want to be wrapped
inside the american flag.
there will be small kettles
of food my mother prepared
around my body.   i will be
so proud you will feel as
if it was really intended.
my brothers are flag toles
and soon songs will flow
me into them.   no one is going
to cry because they never
really knew me.   when the old
men lower me into the earth
one tear will appear on
a side of my eye.   it will
roll a little ways and then stop.

ONE CHIP OF HUMAN BONE

One chip of human bone.

it is almost fitting
to die on the railroad tracks.
i can easily understand
how they felt on their
staggered walks back.

there is something about
trains, drinking, and being
an indian with nothing to lose.

A bible opens then closes real hard
down the dirt road. The wind from the slam
tells a story of a preacher who mumbles far
away from the Church because he has read
the good words to his children
and he listened.

Indians at the gathering sing songs
so that young boys are protected from
death on lands across the oceans.
Six who died stand and whisper
these words songs never crossed the oceans. . . .

The red fox hears this and turns running
with his front feet over his eyes
so the sun does not blind him.
In the morning he will drown
under the icy waters of the river
that was not there four days ago.

They said a naked brown baby
without arms crawled from under
the flag and shouted obscenities
to the cloudless grey sky.

The thin bird flew high above
the reaching old tree starving for wind.
A small boy began to chop the tree
because the shack needed firewood
so his mother would die in warmth.

The fences shivered throughout the night
and on the wire were hawks that
flew after the sun.
In the morning
the thin bird cried when he
found corn under the wet snow. . . .

the blueness of night
grows quietly whispering
at each thought
you have heard of the rock
which lies over fog.
we are almost so magic
and i breathe wings
that brush the smoke
disappearing inside bodies.
below the river is day
clear and rushing faster.
it swallows the meaning
of moon and people
quiet within the pines
killing four sleeping robins.
a body wrapped in a flag
was never seen as glory
until our father asked us
to help even when we were
dying. he knew of these
colors and never asked for
reasons. earth heard them
talking to themselves
far away and always spoke
back: you are home.
the morning came while she
peeled the potatoes for
breakfast and it was then
i felt as a part blending
beautifully but not knowing
where to go.   the rock ate
before us it was given

words by her reminding
our grandfathers to
search for us when the
rain falls and we do not hear.

Biographical Sketches

Paula Allen, a Sioux-Laguna, is a Ph.D. student at the University of New Mexico where she also teaches courses in Native American Literature. Her M.F.A. is from Oregon. "Lament of My Father, Lakota" previously appeared in *The South Dakota Review,* 1973.

Charles G. Ballard is a Quapaw-Cherokee scholar. He taught English at the Chilocco Indian School for seven years and for three years at Northern Oklahoma College, Tonkawa. He is now at Idaho State University. He received his B.A. and M.A. from Oklahoma State University at Stillwater.

Ted Berrigan is of Irish and Choctaw ancestry. Born in Providence, Rhode Island, he received his A.B. and M.A. degrees at the University of Tulsa. He is the editor of "C," *A Journal of Poetry* and of "C" *Press Publications,* as well as critic for *Art News.* His work appears regularly in magazines and reviews and he has published three volumes of poetry. He is widely known for his book *The Sonnets* (Grove Press, 1967) in which "Sonnet XXIII" first appeared.

Harold Bird (Littlebird) is a full-blooded Indian of Santo Domingo and Laguna tribal descent. Born in Albuquerque, New Mexico, he attended public schools in California and Utah. From grades nine through twelve he was a student at the Institute of American Indian Arts, from which he was graduated in 1969. "Death in the Woods" previously appeared in *The American Indian Speaks* (Dakota Press: U. of South Dakota, 1969).

Janet Campbell was born in Riverside, California. She lived on the Coeur d'Alene Reservation in Northern Idaho until she was ten. After a short period on the Colville Reservation in Washington, her family settled on the Yakima Reservation. She attended Wapato (Washington) High School, before going to the Institute of American Indian Arts as a junior. She won a scholarship to the University of California's Novel Writing Workshop. In 1967 she decided to attend City College in San Francisco and in 1969 transferred to the Berkeley campus of the University of California. "Red Eagle" previously appeared in *The South Dakota Review*; "Nespelim Man" previously appeared in *The Whispering Wind,* ed. T.D. Allen, 1972.

Ramona Carden is a member of the Colville tribe. After elementary and high school in Washington, she spent her senior year at the Institute of American Indian Arts. She received her B.A. from Eastern Washington State College. "The Moccasins of An Old Man" and "Tumbleweed" previously appeared in *The Whispering Wind*, ed. T. D. Allen, 1972.

Martha Chosa is from the Pueblo at Jemez. "Drums" previously appeared in *The South Dakota Review*.

Grey Cohoe, Navajo, was born at Shiprock, New Mexico, and attended school there and at Phoenix Indian High School. During his two years at the Institute of American Indian Arts, 1965-67, he won many awards in painting, graphics, and writing. He was granted a scholarship and studied one summer at the Haystack Mountain School of Arts, Deer Isle, Maine. Since then, he has attended the University of Arizona. Grey has been given a one-man show at the university and has been included in many exhibits in this country and in Europe. His etchings and prints are notable for their action and clarity of line. His poem, "The Folding Fan," won first place in the Fifth Annual Vincent Price Awards at the Institute.

Phillip William George, after two years in Vietnam and a long year on the California desert as an Army dental technician, attended Gonzaga University and the University of California, Santa Cruz. He is a member of the Nez Perce Nation at Lapwai, Washington. He spent much of his early life with his maternal great-grandmother, living and learning the ways of his ancestors. He arrived at the Institute of American Indian Arts in the fall of 1964, a graduate of Coulee Dam High School. He was a well-known Indian dance champion of the Pacific Northwest. "Night Blessing" and "Ask The Mountains" previously appeared in *The Whispering Wind*, ed. T. D. Allen, 1972.

Patty Harjo is Seneca-Cayuga-Quapan and studied at the Institute of American Arts. "Musings" previously appeared in *The South Dakota Review*.

Bruce Ignacio was born on the Utah and Duray Reservation in Ft. Duchene, Utah. He attended the Institute of American Indian Arts for three years where he majored in creative writing and jewelry. He exhibited jewelry at the Scottsdale Indian Arts Exhibit in 1971 where he won first prize for his work. He is presently employed in Ft. Duchene, Utah. "Lost" previously appeared in *The South Dakota Review*.

King D. Kuka was born in Browining, Montana. A member of the Blackfeet tribe, he attended high school in Valier, Montana. In 1963 he transferred to the Institute of American Indian Arts, where he studied painting, sculpture, and creative writing. He has won recognition for both his poetry and paintings and sculptures. He is currently attending the University of Montana. "A Taste of Honey" previously appeared in *The Whispering Wind*, ed. T.D. Allen, 1972.

Charles C. Long."Yei-ie's Child" previously appeared in *The Writer's Reader*, ed. T.D. Allen (Institute of American Indian Arts, Santa Fe, New Mexico.)

Alonzo Lopez, Papago, was born in Pima County, Arizona, and attended Sells Consolidated School before entering the Institute of American Indian Arts as a sophomore. He was accepted for an interim year at Yale University when he left the Institute. He successfully completed his work at Yale and was admitted for regular college work, but he elected to transfer to Wesleyan University because curriculum offerings in American Indian Studies at Wesleyan included the Navajo language and other subjects that he desired. "Direction" and "I Am Crying from Thirst" previously appeared in *The South Dakota Review*; "The Lavender Kitten" previously appeared in *The Whispering Wind*, ed. T. D. Allen, 1972.

David Martinez "New Way, Old Way," and "This is Today" both previously appeared in *Anthology of Poetry and Verse by American Indian Art Students* (Department of the Interior, BIA).

Duane McGinnis was born in Seattle, Washington. His mother's tribal affiliation was Klallam, Jamestown band, of which Duane is also a member. He studied at Columbia University and later was graduated from the University of Washington. His first book of poems, *After the Death of and Elder Klallam*, was published in 1970. He has been accepted for graduate school at the Writing Seminars at Johns Hopkins University. "Indian Prayer" and "Train Rhythms and the Color Wheel" were previously published in *Prairie Schooner*; "Song for Yellow Leaf Moon" appeared in *The South Dakota Review*.

Emerson Blackhorse Mitchell was born in a hogan. He attended school at Ignacio, Colorado, until his junior year in high school when he transferred to the Institute of American Indian Arts. His father had died in service in World War II. His maternal grandparents cared for him and gave him his early training in the Navajo way. Barney attended Fort Lewis College, Durango, Colorado, for one year and transferred to Navaho Community College, Many Farms, Arizona. He is now teaching Social Science at the Round Rock School. "I'm really teaching Navajo culture," he says, and he is teaching in the Navajo language which he enjoys. "Miracle Hill" and "The New Direction" previously appeared in *The South Dakota Review*.

N. Scott Momaday is the son of a Kiowa father and Cherokee mother. Besides Vine Deloria, Jr., Momaday is probably the most widely read Indian author. He won the Pulitzer prize in 1969 for his widely acclaimed novel, *House Made of Dawn*. He also published *The Way to Rainy Mountain* in 1969. He holds his Ph.D. from Stanford and is currently a professor in the English department at Stanford University. "Angle of Geese" appeared previously in *Southern Review*; the others printed in this volume all appeared previously in the *New Mexico Quarterly*.

Calvin O'John, Ute-Navajo, was born in Denver, Colorado. He attended elementary school in Colorado before going to the Institute of American Indian Arts, where he was graduated in 1967. Beside being a poet, his paintings are widely exhibited, lauded by such authorities as the Curator of the Museum of Modern Art, N.Y. "Dancing Teepees" previously appeared in *The Whispering Wind*, ed. T.D. Allen, 1972.

Simon Ortiz is of the Acoma Pueblo in New Mexico, and he is editor of the Navajo *Rough Rock News*. He spent a year studying at the University of Iowa in the International Writing Program. "Ten O'clock News," "This Preparation" and "Smoking My Prayers" appeared previously in *The South Dakota Review*; "Relocation" appeared in *The Way: Anthology of American Indian Literature* (Vintage Books, 1972).

Agnes Pratt, Suquamish, was born at Bremerton, Washington. She attended North Kitsap Elementary School at Poulsbo, Washington, and three different high schools: North Kitsap; St. Euphrasia High, Seattle Washington; and the Institute of American Indian Arts, Santa Fe, New Mexico. She stayed on at the Institute for two years of graduate work. "Death Takes Only a Minute" and "Empathy" previously appeared in *Literary Cavalcade*, 1969.

Fred Red Cloud, a Denver businessman, is Seneca by descent. He is one of the editors of the *Mustang Review*, a semi-annual poetry magazine. "A Tale of Last Stands" appeared previously in the *Prairie Schooner*, 1970; "Machu Picchu, Peru" appeared in *Epoch*, 1971.

Ronald Rodgers was born at the Indian Hospital in Claremore, Oklahoma. He is a member of the Cherokee Nation. At fifteen, he entered the Institute of American Indian Arts as a sophomore. His major interest became writing, particularly short stories. He also developed an aptitude for drama and acted several major roles in school and community performances. In his junior year at IAIA, Ron won a second place in the nationwide Scholastic Awards and his short story, "The Good Run," appeared in *Cavalcade* magazine for January, 1967. Ron attended San Francisco State college during the 1968-69 Hayakawa-hiatus year, wrote on his own one term, and transferred mid-term, 1970, to UCLA. He thereafter transferred to the University of California at Santa Cruz. "Taking Off" appeared previously in *The South Dakota Review;* "Kindergarten" previously appeared in *The Whispering Wind,* ed. T. D. Allen, 1972.

Norman Russell is of Cherokee ancestry and is a professor of biology at Central State College, Edmund, Oklahoma. His first book of poems, *At the Zoo,* was published in 1969. "The World Has Many Places, Many Ways" and "The Eyes of the Child Do Not See Me" appeared previously in *Southwest Review;* "The Great Way of the Man" and "Clerks Song II" appeared in *The South Dakota Review.*

Bruce Severy was born in Santa Monica, California. He did undergraduate work at Washington State University before graduating from the University of California, Long Beach. He also did graduate work there. Severy has been widely published in such journals as *Dakotah Territory, Prairie Schooner, Cafe Solo, Measure, Pinache, the Outsider,* and others. He is currently teaching English, Journalism and Drama at Drake High School in Drake, North Dakota.

Loyal Shegonee is from the Potawatomi tribal group. "Loneliness" appeared previously in *The South Dakota Review.*

Liz Sohappy was given in 1969 her Palouse name, Om-na-ma, which was that of her great-grandmother on her father's side. She says of this: "My Indian name has made a great difference in my life. I really felt like a floating body until I recieved my name. My grandmother said that is how it was to be—no one is here on earth until he has an Indian name." Liz attended the Institute of American Indian Arts for most of two years and then studied art in Portland, Oregon, for a time. "Once Again" appeared previously in *The South Dakota Review.*

Soge Track is a Sioux-Pueblo from Taos. She was a student at the Institute of American Indian Arts. "Indian Love Letter" appeared previously in *The South Dakota Review.*

Marnie Walsh is a native of Dacotah Territory. She received her B.A. in history, B.A. in English and her M.A. in English, Creative Writing, from the

University of New Mexico. "Vickie" and "Bessie Dreaming Bear" were previously published by *Dacotah Territory* (Moorhead State College, Minnesota); "Thomas Iron-eyes," "Seth Dismounts Thrice," "Charlie Twohead," and "Emmet Kills Warrior" are published here for the first time.

Winifred Fields Walters is part Choctaw, but says that she knows the Navajo, Zuni and Hopi much better than her own tribe. She lives in Gallup, New Mexico. "Navajo Signs" appeared previously in *The South Dakota Review*.

Archie Washburn was born at Shiprock, New Mexico. He is of Navajo ancestry. He is now a student at Intermountain School in Brigham City, Utah. "Hogan" and "Unknown Smoke" appeared previously in *The South Dakota Review*.

James Welch was born on a Blackfoot reservation in Browning Montana. His father is Blackfeet and his mother is Gros Vendre. He received his B.A. from the University of Montana. He has worked as a laborer, a forest service employee, an Indian firefighter, and a counselor for Upward Bound at the University of Montana; he now devotes full time to writing. He has published in several magazines, including *Poetry, Poetry Northwest*, the *New Yorker, New American Review, The South Dakota Review*, and has also had several works anthologized. *Riding the Earthboy, 40*, his first book of poems, was published in 1971. "One More Time" and "The Man from Washington" appeared previously in *The South Dakota Review;* "Dreaming Winter" and "Harlem, Montana" appeared in *Poetry*.

Donna Whitewing was born in Sutherland, Nebraska. Her father was a farm hand and migrant worker during most of her growing-up years. The family roaded from South Dakota to Nebraska. Donna attended various elementary schools in Nebraska and, on leaving St. Augustine's Indian Mission at Winnebago, received a scholarship to attend Assumption Academy, Norfolk, Nebraska. Donna continues to write as well as work in the Children's Theatre in Winnebago. "August 24, 1963" appeared previously in *The South Review;* "A Vegetable, I Will Not Be" previously appeared in *The Whispering Wind*, ed. T. D. Allen, 1972.

Ray Young Bear was born in Tama, Iowa. His tribe is Sauk and Fox. The poems printed here all appeared previously in *Pembroke Magazine*.

Biographical material for: Harold Bird (Littlebird), Janet Campbell, Ramona Carden, Grey Cohoe, Phillip William George, Patty Harjo, Bruce Ignacio, King D. Kuka, Charles C. Long, Alonzo Lopez, David Martinez, Emerson Blackhorse Mitchell, Calvin O'John, Agnes Pratt, Ronald Rogers, Loyal Shegonee, Liz Sohappy, and Dona Whitewing is used by permission of T.D. Allen and the Institute of American Indian Arts, Sante Fe, New Mexico, a Bureau of Indian Affairs School.